D1179373

The Little Book of Monarchs

English History with a Smile on Its Face

with best wishes,

Tony Boullemier.

Tony Boullemier

Illustrated by Adrian Teal

Matador
9 Priory Business Park
Kibworth Beauchamp
Leicestershire LE8 0RX, UK
Tel: (+44) 116 279 2299
Fax: (+44) 116 279 2277
Email: books@troubador.co.uk
Web: www.troubador.co.uk/matador

ISBN 978 1783060 856

British Library Cataloguing in Publication Data.
A catalogue record for this book is available from the British Library.

Typeset in Calibri by Troubador Publishing Ltd
Printed and bound in the UK by TJ International, Padstow, Cornwall

Matador is an imprint of Troubador Publishing Ltd

Introduction

History is having to fight for its place on the school curriculum against a host of modern subjects.

Many children are only taught the subject through disconnected 'topics'.

I think that's a great pity so I have tried to put it right with *The Little Book of Monarchs.* I have condensed each reign down to the most important events and tried to link each monarch to the next, to show how England has progressed from the brutal but effective dictatorship of William the Conqueror to the much-admired constitutional monarchy of Elizabeth II.

Illustrator Adrian Teal and I have kept our eyes open for the humorous and the peculiar to make it easier for readers to remember who's who.

And we hope this book encourages everyone to delve further into the incredible lives of England's monarchs – men and women who have made our country what it is today.

Tony Boullemier

For my parents,
Lucien and Edith Boullemier,
who first encouraged my
life-long interest in history

ALSO BY TONY BOULLEMIER:

Leonie and the last Napoleon
(Matador)

Contents

House of York

The Tudors

The Stuarts

The Commonwealth

The Stuarts Restored

The Hanoverians 79

House of Saxe-Coburg-Gotha 93

House of Windsor 97

The Normans

William I
William II
Henry I
Stephen

"What exactly is <u>is</u> 'bureaucracy', anyway? Sounds expensive..."

William I

1066 - 1087
The Conqueror

A ruthless Norman general who seized Anglo-Saxon England at Hastings with just 6,000 troops.

Built around 500 castles. Killed or made homeless 150,000 rebels when he laid waste to the north of England.

Initiated the Domesday Book, surveying every settlement so he knew exactly what he could tax.

Introduced feudalism and imposed strict Roman Catholic orthodoxy on the Anglo-Saxon Church.

When he died, his rotting body burst open as it was put in a coffin that was too small for it.

William II

1087 - 1100
William Rufus

The Conqueror's third and favourite son. He never married, had no children and was probably gay.

Ruddy, freckled complexion. Bad tempered and widely unpopular with his nobles and especially the Church.

Brutally suppressed several uprisings by his Norman barons, including his brother Robert.

Beat off two Scottish invasions, killing the King of Scotland in the process.

Killed by an arrow while hunting in the New Forest. Very possibly not an accident.

Henry I

1100 - 1135

White Ship of Woe

Grabbed his dead brother's crown suspiciously quickly and was crowned three days after Rufus's death.

Could read and write, unlike his father William and three brothers.

Feared his elder brother Robert would usurp the throne so he imprisoned him for life.

Fathered as many as 50 illegitimate children but his one legitimate son drowned in the White Ship disaster.

Died from a duodenal ulcer combined with eating 'a surfeit of lampreys' (eels).

"Oi! Knock it off, Matilda!"

Stephen

1135 - 1154

When Anarchy Ruled

Henry nominated Matilda, his last legitimate child, as his heir. But in such warlike times, his barons wanted a king.

So her cousin Stephen, an able soldier, came over from Normandy and seized the throne.

He was pious and popular but too weak to control the barons, which sparked a 19-year civil war with Matilda.

Called 'The Great Anarchy', it brought so much misery to England it was said that "Christ and the saints slept".

Neither side prevailed, but the barons finally forced Stephen to concede succession to his cousin, Henry of Anjou.

The Plantagenets

Henry II
Richard I
John
Henry III
Edward I
Edward II
Edward III
Richard II

12   Henry II

Henry II

1154 - 1189

Emperor of Western Europe

Strongman who ruled an empire that stretched from the Scottish border to the Pyrenees.

His legal reforms included trial by jury and a limit on the power of Church courts.

Fell out with Archbishop Thomas Becket over this, leading to four of his knights assassinating Becket.

He was the first king to invade Ireland and was accepted as its overlord.

Three of his sons rebelled against him and when his wife Eleanor backed them, he imprisoned her for 16 years.

Richard 1

1189 - 1199

The Absentee King

The 6ft 5ins 'Lionheart' was an inspiring general and crusader who spent just seven months of his reign in England.

He appeared to prefer men but married Princess Berengaria of Navarre, who never set foot in her realm at all.

The Third Crusade won safe passage for pilgrims to Jerusalem before he fell out with his French and German allies.

Captured on the journey home, he was ransomed by the German Emperor for £100,000, a huge sum for the times.

Had himself re-crowned in London but then left for France and was killed by an arrow while besieging a castle.

"You've gotta protect me! I could lose my family jewels to a French Count!"

John

1199 - 1216

Born Loser

Richard's brother. Stole his second wife - who was only 12 - from a French count. This provoked war with France.

Lost Normandy and most of his other lands in France. Then he lost his crown jewels while fording quicksands in The Wash.

He was excommunicated by the Pope, who went on to close all of England's churches.

His barons made him seal the Magna Carta but he retracted his promises, triggering civil war and a French invasion.

Did England a favour when he died of dysentery. This united his subjects who then drove out the French.

Henry III

1216 - 1272

Hapless Henry

John's son. He succeeded to the throne when he was only nine and ruled weakly for 56 years.

When he was 20, he replaced his regents with foreign advisors, causing a baronial revolt.

Baron Simon de Montfort imprisoned him and summoned the first parliament to include town representatives.

When the barons fell out, Henry's son Edward defeated de Montfort at Evesham and restored his father's crown.

Kept leopards in his zoo at the Tower of London and promoted scholarship at Oxford and Cambridge.

"Come on, then, if you think you're hard enough..."

Edward I

1272 - 1307

Hammer of the Scots

A merciless and very lucky general, he invaded and conquered Wales.

Twice subdued Scotland – although only temporarily – and had William Wallace executed.

Expelled the Jews to raise money and introduced hanging, drawing and quartering as punishment for treason.

Erected 12 large, ornate crosses between Leicester and London in memory of Eleanor, his dead queen.

Convened a 'Model Parliament' with every borough represented. Died of dysentery while invading Scotland for the third time.

"Sounds like the King has just been demoted to Prince of Wails!"

Edward II

1307 - 1327
A Terrible Death

Following his father's conquest of the country, he was named as the First Prince of Wales.

He fathered four children but preferred men, like his favourites Piers Gaveston and Hugh Despenser.

Lost the Battle of Bannockburn to Robert the Bruce and conceded Scottish independence.

Deposed by 'The She-Wolf of France', his plotting wife Isabella, and her lover Roger Mortimer.

Imprisoned and murdered in Berkeley Castle by having a red hot poker thrust into his bowels.

Edward III

1327 - 1377

Hammer of the French

Formidable soldier and respected reformer who made English the language of courts and Parliament.

When he asserted his claim to the French throne this started the 100 Years' War.

He had great victories at Crecy and Poitiers, capturing the French king. Also seized Scotland's king in a border battle.

England became rich, with booty from innumerable raids on France and from Frenchmen held to ransom.

The Black Death (1349-50) killed one third of the population but enabled serfs to move around the deserted countryside for better wages.

Richard II

1377 - 1399
Died of Starvation

Became king aged 10. His Poll Tax and plans to stops serfs moving about for work, led to the Peasants' Revolt.

He negotiated with its leaders to end the revolt. But then broke his promises and later executed them.

Fell out with his baronial supporters and foolishly exiled Henry Bolingbroke, heir to the Duke of Lancaster.

Became increasingly tyrannical and when Bolingbroke returned to claim his dukedom, he seized the throne as well.

Bolingbroke imprisoned him in Pontefract Castle where he died. Probably left to starve to death.

House
of
Lancaster

Henry IV
Henry V
Henry VI

Henry IV

1399 - 1413

Bolingbroke

Wracked with guilt at having usurped Richard, his reign was plagued by French raids and internal uprisings.

He executed the rebellious Archbishop of York and killed Northumberland's heir, Harry Hotspur, at Shrewsbury.

Defeated Owen Glyndwr, the last Welsh Prince of Wales, who had led a 10-year revolt against him.

A patron of the great poet Geoffrey Chaucer, who wrote wonderfully in English rather than French, the language of the ruling class.

He died prematurely of an appalling skin disease – leprosy, dermatitis or syphilis.

Henry V

1413 - 1422

Hero of Agincourt

Survived a horrendous arrow wound in the face at Shrewsbury to become an inspirational commander and king.

Resumed the 100 Years' War. Won the Battle of Agincourt on St Crispin's Day 1415 and recaptured Normandy.

Forced the defeated French King Charles VI to accept him as his heir.

But he died of dysentery and possibly cancer before he could succeed to the French throne.

Saddled his young son and heir with insoluble problems in trying to hold onto his lands in France.

" The King wants a proper job doing — none of this undercooked French rubbish! "

Henry VI

1422 - 1461

Hopeless Henry

Became king when he was 10 months old. He was always pious and in contrast to his father, very weak.

Lost all of England's remaining lands in France, apart from the area around the important port of Calais.

Had Joan of Arc, who had inspired a French military revival, burned at the stake on trumped-up heresy charges.

Suffered severe mental breakdowns which led to Richard Duke of York being named 'Protector of England'.

On his recovery, he refused to let York join his Lancastrian-dominated council and the Wars of the Roses started.

House
of
York

Edward IV
Edward V
Richard III

Edward IV

1461 - 1483
Won Back his Throne

Duke Richard's son. He beat Henry's Lancastrians at Mortimers Cross and then Towton to secure the throne.

Secretly married Elizabeth Woodville but her many ambitious relatives infuriated his ally the Earl of Warwick.

Warwick changed sides, drove King Edward into exile and restored Henry VI to the throne.

But Edward returned, killing Warwick at Barnet, Henry's son at Tewkesbury and Henry in the Tower of London.

Had his own treacherous brother, the Duke of Clarence, drowned in a butt of malmsey wine in the Tower.

"Stop whining! I bought you a tin of fudge from the gift shop, didn't I?!"

Edward V

1483

Prince in the Tower

Succeeded to his father's throne at 12, but was waylaid en route to London by his uncle Richard, Duke of Gloucester.

He and his brother were put in The Tower 'for their own protection' by the Duke.

Seen playing in the garden and then spotted at the windows. But after a few weeks, they were never seen again.

Gloucester had their father's marriage declared to be invalid and the Princes therefore illegitimate.

Shortly afterwards the Duke of Gloucester had himself crowned as Richard III.

Richard III

1483 - 1485

Killed at Bosworth

Edward IV's brother. Good general and energetic administrator, popular in the north but not the south and London.

Although suspected of murdering the Princes, this has never been proved and may have been Tudor propaganda.

The last English king to die in battle when part of his army betrayed him to Henry Tudor's rebels at Bosworth Field.

In 2012 his skeleton was unearthed at the site of a friary in nearby Leicester, revealing he had curvature of the spine.

This was what made Shakespeare describe him as a hunchback. But there's no proof he cried: "My kingdom for a horse".

The Tudors

Henry VII
Henry VIII
Edward VI
Lady Jane Grey
Mary I
Elizabeth I

Henry VII

1485 - 1509
First Tudor

Lancastrian Henry had a poor claim to the throne but by marrying Elizabeth of York he united the rival factions.

Won the last battle of the Wars of the Roses at Stoke Field and then broke the barons' power by banning private armies.

Dour, manipulative and suspicious, but he set England's finances and legal system straight.

Beset by rebellions and pretenders, he would have had the most to gain from killing the Princes in the Tower.

A patron of England's first printer, William Caxton, he encouraged a revival of learning.

"The lord giveth, and the lord taketh away!"

Henry VIII

1509 - 1547

Despot with Six Wives

**Married six times in search of a healthy male heir –
divorced, beheaded, died, divorced, beheaded, survived.**

Broke away from Rome and set up a reformed Church of
England with himself as its head.

**His huge naval expansion, Scottish wars and sabre rattling
at France helped empty his exchequer.**

Dissolved 800 monasteries and abbeys, grabbing their
wealth and becoming widely hated.

**Executed tens of thousands of his subjects for rebelling or
protesting over religion and taxes.**

Edward VI

1547 - 1553

Boy King

Henry VIII's sickly and only legitimate son, by Jane Seymour, he succeeded aged nine.

Ruled with the help of two regents, the Dukes of Somerset and Northumberland.

He was a kind and sensitive boy who hated burning Catholic heretics at the stake.

But he strengthened the Reformation, banning Catholic Mass and introducing the new prayer book.

Named his Protestant cousin Jane Grey as his successor and died aged 15 of tuberculosis.

"Nice crown. I hope they kept the receipt!"

Lady Jane Grey

1553
Nine day Queen

A highly intelligent girl, she was married to the Duke of Northumberland's son.

Fourth in line, she was pushed onto the throne to prevent Catholic Princess Mary succeeding.

Her supporters failed to capture Mary or to stop her staging a counter-coup.

Jane's reign lasted only nine days after her proclamation, when Mary persuaded the Privy Council to side with her.

She was later executed on Mary's orders, along with Northumberland.

"And now they're blaming me for Calais..."

Mary I

1553 - 1558

Bloody Mary

A devout Catholic, like her mother Catherine of Aragon, she sought close ties with Rome again.

Repealed much pro-Protestant legislation and had Queenship made legally equal to Kingship.

She married Philip of Spain and but there were no children from their four-year marriage.

Had nearly 300 Protestants, including Archbishop Cranmer and Bishops Latimer and Ridley, burned at the stake.

Lost Calais, England's remaining possession in France and claimed its name would be found engraved on her heart.

" They won't get far, gentlemen — I've heard the Shipping Forecast! "

Elizabeth I

1558 - 1603

Virgin Queen

Henry's daughter established non-zealous Protestantism and executed hundreds of Catholics on treason charges.

Beset by plots to put her Catholic cousin Mary Queen of Scots on the throne, she finally executed her too.

This led to the Spanish Armada, defeated by Howard of Effingham, Francis Drake and bad weather at sea.

Her intrepid sailors, explorers and colonists laid the foundation for Britain's overseas empire and prosperity.

She never wed and insisted it was better being 'married to my country'.

The
Stuarts

James I
Charles I

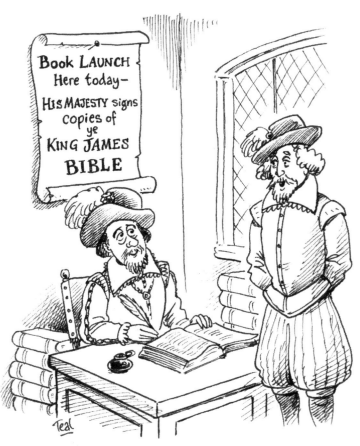

"Could you make it out to 'My close personal friend Buckingham,' please?"

James I

1603 - 1625
Wisest Fool

Elizabeth's cousin, King James VI of Scotland, he united the crowns of England, Ireland and Scotland.

Nicknamed the 'Wisest Fool in Christendom', he seldom washed and wore padded clothes for fear of assassins.

Probably bi-sexual and famed for slobbering over favourites like Somerset and Buckingham.

Principal target of The Gunpowder Plot, intended to blow up Parliament and trigger a Catholic uprising.

King James Bible introduced; Shakespeare's career reached its height; and colonists founded Jamestown, Virginia in America.

Charles I

1625 – 1649
Lost his Head

James's son, he believed in a king's divine right and ruled without Parliament during the 'Eleven-year Tyranny'.

His Catholic wife was unpopular. And some advisors, like Buckingham who was assassinated, were hated.

His new prayerbook started war with the Scots. Then Parliament refused to grant him money without reforms.

Civil War broke out and one in four Englishmen fought. Charles and his 'Cavalier' followers lost, despite his queen pawning jewels for funds.

He was captured but conspired with the Scots to get his throne back. Tried and sentenced to death by one vote.

The

Commonwealth

Lord Protector Cromwell

Cromwell

1649 -1660

Repression and Depression

Oliver Cromwell, a masterful general, was elected Protector and brutally subdued risings in Scotland and Ireland.

Cromwell rejected the crown as his 'Roundhead' followers tried new ways of ruling to replace the monarchy.

He defeated the exiled Charles II at Worcester and raised English military prestige in Europe and the West Indies.

But the Roundheads' repression of fun, such as closing the theatres, caused widespread unrest.

Cromwell's son Richard succeeded him. But General Monk and the army backed a restoration of the monarchy.

The
Stuarts

Restored

Charles II
James II
William III & Mary II
Anne

" Ah, Wren — how are you at designing nurseries?"

Charles II

1660 - 1685
Merry Monarch

Charles I's son was put on the throne but came off second best in the naval wars with Holland.

Yet he brought fun back to England, in spite of London's last plague in 1665 and the Great Fire of 1666.

Became a patron of architect Christopher Wren and scientists like Isaac Newton.

Had many mistresses and fathered as many as 16 illegitimate children. But he left no legitimate heir.

He dealt diplomatically with religious unrest, tolerating Catholics and converting to Catholicism on his deathbed.

James II

1685 - 1689

Catholic Abdicator

Brother of Charles II, he crushed Monmouth's rebellion at the Battle of Sedgemoor followed by 'The Bloody Assizes'.

But tactlessly he planned to return Britain to Catholic ways.

Protestants were alarmed when his Catholic wife had a son, alleged to be an orphan, and smuggled in via a warming pan.

Parliament invited James's daughter Mary and her husband, William of Orange, to replace him.

When William landed, James fled to France, allowing the 'Glorious Revolution' to take place bloodlessly.

William III
& Mary II
1689 -1702
Glorious Revolutionaries

They ruled jointly until Mary, who was four and half inches taller than her husband, died of smallpox aged 32.

William defeated an attempted comeback by James II when he won the Battle of the Boyne in Ireland.

The Act of Settlement in 1701 ensured England and Scotland would never again be ruled by a Catholic.

And it was decreed that no monarch could ever again impose taxes or laws without Parliamentary approval.

Their reign saw the Bank of England set up and William died after his horse stumbled on a molehill and threw him.

Anne

1702 -1714

Motherhood Misery

She was Mary's sister and had 18 pregnancies. But none of the children reached adulthood.

Her general, Marlborough, won four stunning victories against France in The War of Spanish Succession.

She presided over the 1705 Act of Parliamentary Union with Scotland.

During her rule, horse-racing started at Ascot in 1711 and the last witch was executed in England in 1712.

And the Two-party Parliamentary System with Whigs and Tories was developed in the House of Commons.

The Hanoverians

George I
George II
George III
George IV
William IV
Victoria

George I

1714 -1727

First Hanoverian

A German prince and Anne's nearest Protestant relative, he succeeded despite 50 Catholics having better claims.

He put down James Stuart's 1715 rebellion in Scotland.

George was unpopular and couldn't speak English. Some blamed him for the 'South Sea Bubble' financial crisis.

As the monarchy's influence waned, Robert Walpole became effectively Britain's first Prime Minister.

Hanoverian London was summed up in Hogarth's paintings, symbolising ruination and death through gin drinking.

George II

1727 - 1760

Last Royal Commander

George l's son and the last English king to lead an army into battle – victory against France at Dettingen in 1743.

Put down Bonnie Prince Charlie's 1745 rebellion at Culloden and cleared out the Highland clans.

Jacobite Lord Lovat was the last public beheading in 1746 and witchcraft was abolished as a crime.

He added India and Canada to his empire and his Royal Charter founded Georgia in America.

George was an enthusiastic patron of composer Handel and finally died sitting on the toilet.

"Keep orf moy land !!"

84   George III

George III

1760 - 1820
Farmer George

George II's grandson. Nicknamed for his common touch, which helped stop French revolutionary fever spreading to England.

By taxing American colonists without their having representation, he lost America in the War of Independence.

Nelson's victory at Trafalgar and Wellington's in the Peninsular War and then at Waterloo, finished Napoleon.

In his reign, Watt developed the steam engine and Captain Cook claimed Australia and other lands for Britain.

He went mad three times through porphyria and his son, the future George IV, acted as Regent for his final nine years.

George IV

1820 - 1830
Prince Regent

He was fat, dissolute and wildly extravagant and had numerous mistresses.

A patron of architecture and the arts, his reign saw the National Gallery established.

He secretly married Catholic Mrs Fitzherbert and had to be persuaded by Parliament to give her up.

Then pushed into marrying Caroline of Brunswick. When they parted unhappily, he barred her from his coronation.

Trade unions were legalised in his reign and the Railway Age began at Stockton and Darlington.

William IV

1830 - 1837
Silly Billy

Eccentric brother of George IV. He stopped his carriage to give strangers a lift on the day he became king.

Joined the Navy at 13, he was a friend of Nelson and a kidnap target for George Washington's American rebels.

Prime Minister Wellington made him resign as Lord High Admiral for vanishing at sea with his squadron for 10 days.

Reformed our unrepresentative Parliament. Abolished colonial slavery and factory work by children under nine.

David Cameron is descended from one of the 10 illegitimate children he had with his mistress Dorothy Jordan.

"You did mail the invitation, didn't you?"

Victoria

1837 - 1901

Empress of India

Her empire covered a quarter of the world thanks to the army, railways, steamships and industrialisation.

She was titled Empress of India but never visited. Ended centuries of French hostility by befriending Napoleon III.

Had nine children by Prince Albert. But her over-long mourning after his early death, made her unpopular.

Extended voting franchise. Repealed the Corn Laws to lower bread prices. Made primary education compulsory.

Survived seven assassination attempts and reigned for 63 years 216 days - our second longest reigning monarch.

House of Saxe-Coburg-Gotha

Edward VII

Edward VII

1901 - 1910
Prince of Fun

A philandering socialite who re-popularised the monarchy with massive shows of pageantry.

His coronation had to be postponed for a dangerous operation on a stomach abscess.

He shunned snobbery and became a symbol of national unity by reaching out to ordinary people.

Famed for numerous mistresses including Alice Keppel, great grandmother of Prince Charles's wife Camilla.

Wisely pressed for naval expansion, to counter the military build-up of his nephew, Germany's Kaiser William.

House

of
Windsor

George V
Edward VIII
George VI
Elizabeth II

"The Kaiser's a pussy-cat compared
with <u>this</u> fella!"

George V

1910 - 1936

B***er Bognor!

Called his cousin, Kaiser William, 'the greatest criminal ever' for starting World War I.

Refused to allow his relatives, the Russian royals, to escape their revolution and live in England.

Scarcely read a book and shot more than a million game birds. But hard-working, popular and shrewd.

Guided the Monarchy through Irish independence, the General Strike and women over 21 getting the vote.

On his deathbed, his last words to an aide proposing a restorative seaside outing, were, allegedly: 'B***er Bognor'.

Edward VIII

1936

Abdicated for Mrs Simpson

As a prince visiting an impoverished Welsh mining village, he popularly declared: 'Something must be done.'

His father George V predicted: 'After I am dead, the boy will ruin himself in 12 months'.

He did so. A playboy who admired Hitler's Nazi Germany, he became a disastrous monarch.

Facing the choice of remaining king or marrying American divorcee Wallis Simpson, he abdicated.

Made Duke of Windsor, he was sent to govern the Bahamas during World War II. Thereafter, he lived in Paris.

George VI

1936 - 1952

Braved the Blitz

Edward's young brother, he was bottom of the class at naval college but fought at sea in the 1916 Battle of Jutland.

A shy introvert, he had to be tutored into losing his stammer when he made speeches and the first radio broadcasts.

Throughout The Blitz during World War II, he braved the German bombing raids by staying in London.

Became the first king to fly and was the figurehead of British hopes and resistance to Nazi invasion efforts.

His reign saw the creation of the National Health Service and independence granted to India.

Elizabeth II

1952 -

Our Longest Ruler

On September 9th 2015 she became our longest ruler, overtaking Victoria's 63 years 216 days.

Highly-respected and popular head of state in 16 countries and figurehead of a 53-member Commonwealth.

Her troops have fought in Aden, Kenya, Cyprus, Egypt, Northern Ireland, the Falklands, Iraq and Afghanistan.

1992 was her 'annus horribilis' when three of her children divorced or separated and Windsor Castle caught fire.

She has seen Everest climbed, hanging ended, Beatlemania, decimalisation, our first female premier and a stunning London Olympic Games.

Those royal families

The Normans

They were Vikings from Scandinavia who settled in North West France and were eventually given this land by the French king. It became known as Normandy and Duke William was its ruler when he invaded England and seized its crown in 1066.

The Plantagenets

William the Conqueror's youngest son, Henry I, had a daughter named Matilda. She married a Norman-French baron named Geoffrey Plantagenet and their son became Henry II, the first Plantagenet king.

The House of Lancaster

The Plantagenet family evolved into two rival branches striving for power. The Lancastrian branch gave England three kings and the incompetence of the last one, Henry VI, caused what became known as the Wars of the Roses.

The House of York

This was the other Plantagenet branch, which also provided three kings. The last one, Richard III, became the last English king to die in battle.

The Tudors

King Henry V's widow had remarried a Welsh courtier named Owen Tudor. Their grandson Henry Tudor thus had a slim claim to the throne. He invaded England, killed Richard III in battle, seized the crown and founded the Tudor dynasty.

The Stuarts

Queen Elizabeth I, the last Tudor monarch, died childless so she passed the throne on to her cousin James, the king of Scotland and a member of the Stuart family.

The Commonwealth

This was England's short-lived experiment of doing without a monarch. After executing King Charles I, the republicans styled their leader Oliver Cromwell as 'Lord Protector'. His son succeeded him on his death. But in a very short time the Stuarts were invited back.

The Hanoverians

Queen Anne, the last Stuart monarch, died without an heir and since the Constitution now decreed that only a Protestant could rule England, the crown passed to her closest Protestant relative, Prince George, ruler of the German state of Hanover.

Saxe-Coburg-Gotha

This was the house of Prince Albert, husband and consort to Queen Victoria. When she died, their son Edward VII inherited the crown under the name of this house.

The Windsors

The Saxe-Coburg-Gotha name, with its German connotation, was dropped in 1917 during the bitterness of World War One. The royal family changed its name to Windsor after the castle where they lived.

HISTORY QUIZ

How much do you remember? Here are 20 questions to test your knowledge

1. Which king is David Cameron descended from?
2. Who did Queen Mary I marry?
3. Which king wore padded clothes in fear of assassination?
4. Which was the last English king to die in battle?
5. Who made friends with France after hundreds of years of hostilities?
6. Who was ruling when the last witch was executed in England?
7. Which king was four and half inches shorter than his queen?
8. Whose reign was so miserable it was said that "Christ and the saints slept"?
9. How many troops did William the Conqueror have at the Battle of Hastings?
10. Which was the first king to invade Ireland and be accepted as its overlord?
11. How did King Edward ll die?
12. How many countries does Queen Elizabeth ll have in her Commonwealth?

13. How many of his subjects was King Henry VIII said to have put to death?

14. Who spent only seven months of his 10-year reign in England?

15. Who summoned the first Parliament to include representatives of towns?

16. Which king is said to have had as many as 50 illegitimate children?

17. Who was drowned in a butt of Malmsey wine in the Tower of London?

18. Who fell out with the Pope, causing all of England's churches to be closed?

19. Name two kings who went mad during their reigns.

20. Which king starved to death in Pontefract Castle?

ANSWERS:

1 William IV; 2 Philip of Spain; 3 James I; 4 Richard III; 5 Victoria; 6 Anne; 7 William III; 8 Stephen; 9 Six thousand; 10 Henry II; 11 Red hot poker in the bowels; 12 Fifty-three; 13 Tens of thousands; 14 Richard I; 15 Simon de Montfort; 16 Henry I; 17 The Duke of Clarence; 18 John; 19 Henry VI and George III; 20 Richard II.

Acknowledgements

The author compiled this little book after a lifetime of reading histories, biographies and historical novels too numerous to list.

But he would like to give special thanks to illustrator Adrian Teal for his unique cartoons. And he is indebted to the advice of medieval expert and author David Baldwin of Leicester University, whose fascinating lectures he has been attending for 17 years.

He found further inspiration from numerous battlefield visits with Holts Tours, including several brilliantly led by the late Professor Richard Holmes.

He is grateful to journalists Caroline Compton and Kerry Boullemier and teachers Chet Chebegia, Elwyn and Janet Lewis, Ronald and Jean Scholes, Chris Pickett, Denise Bott and the children of Boughton School for their help and observations.

He thanks publicist Jacqui MacCarthy for her valuable advice; web designer Aimee Bell and Matador's book designer Terry Compton for their skill and patience; and his dear wife Marie for her endless support.

And finally, he would like to pay tribute to his motivational history teachers at the Royal Grammar School, Newcastle-upon-Tyne, including 'Jabber', 'Wilkie' and 'Happy Ned'.

Happy history days indeed!

Tony Boullemier was born in Newcastle-upon-Tyne in 1945 and worked as a journalist there and in Fleet Street. He started his own newspaper group in Northampton in 1975 and ran it for 14 years before selling out to an international publisher. Married with two children, he lives in Northamptonshire where he follows many sporting interests, studies history and writes. This is his second book.

www.boullemierbooks.co.uk

Illustrator Adrian Teal
www.tealcartoons.com